BEHIND THE EYES
OF A
CANCER
PATIENT

BEHIND THE EYES

OF A

CANCER

PATIENT

Experiences of My Journey

Lakeya Cunningham

Behind the Eyes of a Cancer Patient

ISBN 978-0-578-30989-7

This book is dedicated to Yakima Williams, Deborah Edmonds, my lifelong Pink Sisters, friends, family, and the creator who made it all possible: GOD.

Table of Contents

PART ONE

THE TIRED TRUTH

I have been very tired lately. More than usual. My job is pretty demanding, so I am accustomed to going home worn out at the end of the night. Being a full-time waitress has its share of exhausting days, but this feels a little different. Am I coming down with a cold? Could this be anxiety? Hopefully it isn't anything major.

The other night I felt a lump in my breast, which has me a bit worried. I'm concerned it might be infected. It feels like a piece of coal is stuck in there. I want to get myself checked out, but I can't afford the bill that comes with getting the test done. I don't have insurance, and I'm confronted by too many bills to think about paying for health care out-of-pocket. My sister is a nurse; maybe she can tell me what she thinks it is and I can save my money.

I don't know why I thought it would be a good idea to pick up an extra shift at work today. I found it almost impossible to focus at work. I was wasting drinks on customers, forgetting customer's food orders, and definitely making myself look as if I had no idea what I was doing. My mind was all over the place and I could no longer focus on anything else. It's time I check this thing out. Good or bad or ugly, I need my life back, my thoughts back, and my sanity back in order to focus on the things around me.

Today is her off day. Problem solved. I'll go by her house tonight after work. Hopefully she can give me some answers.

***

The night was like any other in most ways. Although I was tired, I still managed to make my money. In order to catch my sister, I decided to pay my fellow waitress friend to clean my section so I could leave early. I made it in the nick of time. My sister was on her couch cuddled up, getting settled in for the night. She has a lot of stairs to her front door, so as I entered her house, I had to catch my breath before asking her to diagnose me. Once I was seated, I eased my questions in.

"Ummm, so hey Sis, I know you are not a doctor but, I have a lump in my breast and I'm not sure what it is. I figured you would know more than me so I need you to look at it for me."

…

"Listen, I know you are not a doctor, but I assumed you would have an idea of what it is."

…

"You sure you can't diagnose me? Ok, ok, ok. If I'm not feeling more energetic after my shift tomorrow,

I'll take an afternoon off and get it checked out. I'll call in the morning and see if I can make an appointment for a mammogram."

The next morning, I was up early. I didn't want to miss work because it was the first of the month and my bills were all due so I needed to work. I decided to call the clinic and schedule an appointment for sometime the following week if possible so I could preplan taking time off work.

The phone rang for a long time, and finally a lady picked up.

"Hello ma'am, I am calling to schedule a mammogram for myself. I feel a lump and I'm afraid it may be serious. Do you guys take walk-ins?"

The lady repeated most of my questions.

"Yes ma'am, walk-ins. I am thirty-one years old."

...

"Yes ma'am, thirty-one."

...

"What do you mean?! So you're telling me I am too young to refer myself for a mammogram? What if I really need one?"

...

"I have to go through my doctor? What if I don't have a doctor, ma'am?"

...

"So there is nothing you can do for me?"

Wow! What an outdated system!

"Now how will I get a mammogram?" I asked myself, as I hung up on the phone.

I was furious that I wasn't able to refer myself, regardless of whether it was just a scare or not. I should have the right to get checked out, right? Now I was even more determined to get a mammogram even though the reason as to why I thought I needed one was minor. At this point, it was the principle. I wanted a mammogram more than ever, now.

Come on, think, Lakeya. How can you get a mammogram at your age with no insurance?

I thought about that big pink bus that drives around town, but it was booked for the next two weeks. I didn't want to wait that long.

Then I had an idea. I don't know why this was my initial thought, but it seemed like a good idea.

I'll just have to just go to the ER and fake some chest pains to make them take me seriously. Forgive me God, but I need to get some help.

THE NON-EMERGENCY

The same night after work, I decided to go to the ER. The lady at the front door seemed rather inattentive. I was a little relieved thinking maybe she wouldn't pick up on the fact that I wasn't having chest pains at all. I didn't think my acting skills were terribly great, so I could definitely use the extra help of her being distracted!

"Excuse me, ma'am. I'm coming in for chest pains. I am having major chest pains in this area right here," I pointed to the hard spot on my chest. "Can someone please look at it?"

...

"No ma'am, I don't have insurance but I feel horrible."

She pointed to a chair and asked if I could make it to sit down in the chair.

"Yes ma'am, I can. I can wait. Thank you," I told her as I eased myself towards the chair.

The wait wasn't as long as I expected it might be. There were a lot of people with chest pains in the waiting room so I was feeling pretty guilty, but I needed to be taken seriously, and this was the only way I could think of to get the ER staff's attention.

A nurse called me into a room and told me to wait for a doctor to come in. While I waited, she hooked me up to an IV and gave me a heated blanket. I made myself comfortable and was almost asleep when the doctor walked in. I almost forgot why I was there.

He was a tall, tanned, handsome, doctor who looked like he worked out pretty frequently. I was impressed by his physique, but I had to stay focused on the task at hand. He was so easy on the eyes though. I couldn't help but watch him walk around the room in admiration. His smile looked painted on, and his teeth were perfect and pearly white. He asked me a series, of questions but honestly, I had a few of my own. Ha. I noticed there was no ring on his finger, which I'm sure makes his job even harder because women are always on the prowl—women just like myself.

"Focus, Lakeya! You're here for help with this lump, not to find a husband!

I figured in order to get his attention, I had to go all out.

"My pain level from one to ten? It's a ten right now."

...

"No, I don't know what could have brought this on. I just suddenly started feeling pain in my chest right here."

I pointed to the area I needed him to check.

The doctor listened to my heart and pushed down on the area I was complaining about. He felt something as well and decided that I should get a mammogram just to be safe. He assured me he was fairly certain it was nothing to be stressed about due to my age, and it was probably something that required a small fix. Likely a small, benign cyst that could be easily removed.

The doctor ran some tests on me but couldn't confirm or deny any specific diagnosis based off of the tests, so he arranged to send me to a surgeon specialist the next day who could do a biopsy and give me more information. I wasn't happy with having to see a specialist, but I was thrilled that I could finally get someone to pay attention to this weird-feeling spot in my breast and try to find out what was really going on.

***

I ended up going in late to work that next day to make sure I could make the specialist appointment on time. Entering the noticeably busy office, I was immediately irritated. I had to stand in a long line to get checked in, and I was then sent to the waiting room, which was packed. I wasn't a happy camper because I had spent the entire night in the ER, and here I was this morning going through a similar ordeal for something that I might just need an antibiotic to clear up. But I was too invested now not to find out what was happening with this lump. I had to keep going.

After about half an hour, the nurse called me and walked me back to see the doctor. She was friendly and asked me a series of questions about my family's health. After I answered all her questions, she took my blood pressure and told me the doctor would be right in to see me.

"Thank you," I told her as I took a seat on the bed.

Although I was exhausted from all of the chaos of the previous couple of days, I was relieved that the ordeal was almost over and I would soon have some answers. I dozed off, so I'm not sure how long my wait was. When I heard the door open, I hopped up in order to avoid the embarrassment of being caught sleeping.

The surgeon seemed to have not noticed my slumbering. He was preoccupied by something he was writing down about the patient before me. I instantly got the sense he was a serious man and not a man of many words.

As he entered the room, he started asking me a series of questions about my family history of cancer, diabetes, high blood pressure, etc. Although I had already given the nurse all of this information, I felt obligated to answer his questions as well and in a hurried manner. Once he finished writing down notes, he had me prepare for the biopsy by undressing from my waist up and lying back on the bed.

He took samples and told me he would get them sent off right away with the expectation that we should have answers by Monday morning. I was thrilled to have this load taken off of me, but I was so nervous about the possibility of results coming back with the worst news of my life. I knew the lump meant something, but I wasn't sure exactly what. I'm sure that, based on my facial expression, he sensed that I was worried. He assured me that considering my age and ethnicity and with there being no real family history of cancer, I shouldn't have anything to worry about. He told me to forget about the test and to enjoy my weekend. He didn't have to ask me twice!

***

Monday morning, I received a phone call telling me to come into the surgeon's office right away.

"Ma'am, I don't understand why, but I can be there this afternoon before picking my kids up from school. I'll just call my job and let them know I'll be late for my shift."

***

There I was, in the examining room again.

Why is it that we have to wait so long for the doctor when he is the one that sets the appointments? Does an appointment mean anything these days? I grumbled to myself as I waited again. I had literally agreed to a specific appointment time so I could avoid the waiting process.

I felt uncomfortable, alone in this room, and I just wanted to get this over with so I could beat the school traffic, pick up the kids, feed them, get them to after-school activities, and get them started on homework and baths. All I wanted was to truly have one peaceful moment in this long, stressful day.

Oh good! Here he is! Ok, let's make this quick doc so I can ...

…

Wait, what?! Wait, wait, wait, wait, wait, did he just say I have cancer?

…

Wait, this is not how this was supposed to go. Am I losing it? Hold on … let me listen closer to the things that he is saying …

…

Yes, he definitely said "cancer" and "future procedures." He has to be mistaken! I am only thirty-one and I have never even had the flu! It is apparent he has no idea what he is talking about. I should have done my research to find the best doctor in town like I said I would before even agreeing to this test. I'm sure he has made a mistake like this before. I blame myself for not reading the reviews on this place.

I am going to let him finish talking, kindly nod to everything he says, and GET OUT OF HERE!!!!!

I didn't even stop at the check-out desk. I ran as fast as I could to my car.

I don't want anyone to see me like this. I have to get out of here. I have to go!

***

Me?! Cancer?! How?

I could not imagine dealing with cancer.

How could this be happening? What does this mean for my future? Am I going to die?

I have not even really lived my life yet! There is so much that I want to do. Honestly, I have not even left my hometown. I want to go on trips. I want to see the entire world through my eyes, not just what the internet has provided for me. I have yet to buy a house, and I want to be able to leave my kids with a source of stability. Be the provider they are needing, someone to help them for as long as they live. I want to get married and live with the love of my life until I am old. This is not good timing to die!

What do I tell my children? What will they do without me? Who will they live with? Will they be separated? Is it possible for someone to love them as much as I do? There's so much I haven't shown them—so much I haven't told them. Why do they have to watch me die? What did they do to deserve this?

I have to calm down. I can't keep crying like this. I don't want to scare my children. I'll figure this out later.

The school line was long but I was no longer complaining about it. I needed a minute to think.

Maybe he was mistaken. I'll just wait on the phone call with the formal apology.

In order to stay sane, I had to pretend this wasn't happening and try to go on with my day.

It can't be real anyways, right? Besides, I do not have time for this. I have a lot to do. My kids are waiting to tell me all about their day, the dishes need to be washed, and I have a bill due today. I have to remember to get that paid. I'm sure the children's teachers prepared a lot of homework I have to help with. Life is waiting for me. I don't have time to die or even think about dying. Suck it up, Buttercup. Put on your best smile. Here come the kiddos now.

THE FIRST DAY OF THE REST OF MY LIFE

OK, so they didn't call me and tell me they had made a mistake. And I don't understand why I am here again. Maybe they wanted to apologize in person. Seems like a better way for a professional facility to apologize. If it were me, I would apologize in person as well.

At least I know I won't be here as long today. I have a million things to do.

Alright, here he is. I am going to look him directly in the eyes to see how sincere he really is with this major screwup. I'll try not to make him feel bad though, and at least this will all be behind us both.

***

What?! I can't believe he is still going through with this whole cancer thing. What a stubborn man! Just apologize already. YOU WERE WRONG. Let me just bring it up. Maybe he needs some help with how to start this apology.

***

So this was not a mistake? I am really that sick. How in the world did it get to Stage 3?! Who just skips all the other stages?! There are only four stages in total! I am really dying! I am really not going to make it.

***

I consider myself to be a Christian. I talk to God often. I mean, I am sure He hears me, and I know He talks back to me. I do my best to live right and serve God the best way I know how. I consider myself to be a good person. They say the good die young, but I wasn't prepared to be the one to test that theory. I had so much more life to live. I thought cancer was for older people. I was only thirty-one and now diagnosed with Stage 3B breast cancer, and to make matters worse, I

16

was considered triple negative. So not only were odds stacked against me to not survive, but my diagnosis was placed at a triple threat of the medicine not even working.

I was so torn in my decision on how to move forward with this. On one hand, my resilient personality wanted me to know I was not going down without a fight, and on the other hand, the reality was that my situation did not look very promising. But because I am a woman of faith, I had to trust and believe in a complete healing. Not only did I have to believe for myself but for everybody who was counting on me.

Why didn't anyone warn me about this? Why was I the last to know? Why me, God? How could I not know? Why can't I stop crying?

I feel so broken. I feel embarrassed for breaking down like this in this doctor's office. I have nothing left. I am totally empty. I never imagined my ending would be like this. I have no idea of what to do, what to feel.

"Go ahead, Doc. Just turn out the lights and leave me here. I just need a minute …."

Ok, God, I don't know what this is and where it came from, but I need you more than ever. I know I can't do this alone, so Lord, I need you. I am broken. The only thing I have right now is my faith, and I am trusting in you to deliver a miracle. Amen.

I am not sure how and don't know why, but here I am, and I hate to admit it, but I think this is the first day of the rest of my life.

PART TWO

MY GUARDIAN ANGEL

So in a little over two weeks, I'll be starting treatments. I will be considered a cancer patient. Just saying it makes me sick to my stomach....

Between now and then, I have an appointment with a different doctor every day. Pet scans, CAT scans, surgery for something called a port, IVs, finger pricks, medication, and a lot of other procedures and information. I have no idea what half of it means; I don't have enough brain power to wrap my head around it all. I think I am going to be sick.

Lord, how am I going to get through this?

Although I consider myself to be a strong person, I need help. I am lost. Everything the doctors say to me sounds like it's in a foreign language. This process is going to be harder than I thought it would be. I may take my cousin up on her offer of reaching out to this lady she told me about who already survived this. I just don't believe in asking for help, nor do I want to have to depend on anyone. I refuse to be seen in the eyes of others as a helpless person. I am a strong, independent woman. I have fought my way through most of my life problems alone, so what makes this different?

I've never understood how people are just so open to sharing their problems with others, especially strangers. I don't trust the opinions of others. It's hard for me to feel that people are genuine anymore. In most situations people don't have your best interest at heart.

I've seen the movies, and I don't want to be the patient in a group session pouring my heart out to strangers. You know what? I'm not going to call this lady. I don't want to throw my problems on her, and she has already survived, right? She's dealt with her own problems. Why would she want to visit this place again? I'll just handle this one myself. How hard can it be?

***

What was I thinking? There is no way I can handle this alone. Visit after visit to the doctors and I am already exhausted. And I haven't even begun treatments yet. These doctors and I are definitely not speaking the same language, and if I see one more needle this week, I am going to scream! My anxiety level is off the charts!

I have family members I can talk to, but I feel like they don't understand me. It's hard to explain to people who have not experienced my situation for themselves what I am going through. I know they love me and are here for me, but sometimes that isn't enough.

Ok, let me call this lady. What do I have to lose, right? I'll see how she sounds on the phone, and if she isn't genuine, I'll kindly excuse myself from the call and suck it up. But if she is genuine, I could really use her help!

"Hello. This is Lakeya Cunningham. My cousin gave me your name and number and told me to reach out to you about my situation. She said you would be able to help me. If so, I can definitely use the help, but if you cannot, I understand that, too."

Whew, what a relief! This lady is being really nice to me!! If I am being honest, it is kind of refreshing to hear the things that she's telling me. How did she know I needed her to dumb this stuff down? Why didn't I think she would have tricks to get through some of these procedures? I feel kind of silly waiting so long to reach out to her. She is so good at this stuff. I hope she doesn't mind me having so many questions.

I really want to ask her about the brand of medicine I learned about today, "The Red Devil." The name just makes me cringe! Maybe she has insight on what Red Devil really is and the effect it has on your body. Honestly, I am terrified by the name alone. Imagine something called Red Devil being inserted into your body!

What will the chemicals do to me? Will I ever feel normal again? I wonder what this medication feels like when it is inside of me. Is there anything I should prepare my family for?

I have so many questions; I am so glad she's willing to help me with anything that I am needing. I am feeling more prepared for this process from just this conversation alone. Even though I planned to take this journey alone, I am grateful that there are people in this world that are willing to help despite how stubborn I am! I really feel like she was sent to me at just the right moment. From this point on I will acknowledge her as she should be viewed: my guardian angel.

Thank you, God for providing her for me even though I was initially too stubborn to receive the help. Yes, she is definitely my guardian angel!

FIRST SURGERY EVER!

I cannot believe I am up before the crack of dawn preparing myself for surgery. Even though I hardly slept last night, I am not as tired as I imagined I would be. It is amazing how your nerves can fuel your energy. At this point, I think I am more afraid of the feeling of not knowing what to expect than the actual surgery.

I have never needed surgery. Better yet, I have never even been seriously ill! The only sickness I can remember is a stomach virus. Boy, do I wish that I could trade this out for a virus now!

I hope my mom is on time. Weird as it sounds, I don't want to be late. I want to give myself lots of time so that I can take a moment to mentally prepare myself for the entire experience, because I know from this moment on, life will be hectic day after day.

I did my research on this port thing they are connecting to my main artery today. I'm not thrilled at all about the purpose for it, but I guess it is better than having an IV needle continuously jabbed into my arm. I hate that feeling. Even though they count down to help you prepare for the initial poke, you never really get used to it. I'm really hoping they put me to sleep, but I'm also mostly afraid that if they put me to sleep and the anesthetic wears off, I'm going to wake up in the middle of surgery surrounded by doctors. What a horrible feeling that would be!

Welp, there is my mom. She has just pulled up in her car and is blowing her horn for me. Let me take this last look in the mirror.

Self, repeat after me, "YOU GOT THIS! YOU WERE MADE TO WIN! You will not be defeated!

Everything will go as planned, and GOD HAS YOU COVERED AS HE ALWAYS DOES. YOU WILL COME OUT ON TOP!"

Ok, here goes nothing!

***

So here we are. I'm in this stinky, uncomfortable, too-big, hospital gown. I wonder how many people have worn this gown? What kind of detergent do they use to clean these gowns? I don't like the smell of this thing. Let me think about something else before I drive myself crazy.

At least they gave me two heated blankets this time instead of one. It's pretty cold here. Who invented the heated blankets, and are they still alive? I would love to thank them personally for the invention.

Ok, Doctor, come on. I'm anxious to get on with this.

I know I am not the only patient in the hospital, but I think it is more nerve-wracking to play this waiting game than to just get it over with. I want to have a nap, but I feel like I will get my rest during this surgery. Also, I don't want to accidentally wake up during surgery because I took a nap earlier. I think I'll take my chances on just staying awake.

Ok, here he is. Finally, it's 8 a.m. Hopefully I'll be out of here by noon so I can peacefully watch a little TV before the children come home. At least I can get some decent sleep and quiet in the daytime until this process is over.

Wait, what do you mean, we have to do some testing? NO! I thought this was surgery day! I am mentally over testing. I WANT THIS TO BE OVER!!

Ok, calm down, Lakeya. Hold back those tears. The nurse is rolling you out of this room right now so here we go, ready or not.

***

So I'm being rolled down the hall by the sweetest little lady. She's of slight build—she may be about 5'6"—and has beautiful brown hair.

Is it just me or are these conversations weird? I feel like I have to make conversation to keep the silence to a minimum, but everything I say feels forced … so fake.

I also feel like I am too heavy to be pushed around by this little lady. Why don't they hire big strong men with muscles to do this job? Having her push me makes me feel lazy—like I'm not carrying my weight. I really want to get out of this bed and just push it myself but I know I'm not allowed to. Wow, depending on others to do things for you is hard.

Ok, great. Here I am in this hall waiting for yet another doctor. I'm surrounded by other patients, wondering what's going through their heads? An older man beside me is staring at the ceiling. I wonder if he is feeling the same way I am—a little scared but also anxious just to get this over with. Why am I being put through this—having to wait? As if my anxiety level isn't high enough!

Think of a happy place, Lakeya. Think of a happy place. This will soon all be behind you.

Finally, it's my turn. I have been in this hall with nothing but my thoughts for the last thirty minutes. I guess I should have been grateful for that weird conversation with the little lady, right?

Ok, so they are explaining the process of injecting my breast with dye and taking pictures to locate the cancerous cells and lymph nodes. This should be a breeze; at least I am not in that hall anymore.

OMG that is a huge needle! Where in the world does she think she is sticking that thing? I did NOT sign up for this!

Ouch! Why does this dye sting sooooo bad? This is the worst feeling ever! Stop saying you're almost done and take it out already! It feels like someone is literally inserting fire and lava into my breast, and they are spreading. If this is how the rest of the day is going to go, I'm not going to make it. I am exhausted and we've just started.

So from the way the previous doctor explained it, I am going to be lit up like a Christmas tree. The imagery makes me laugh, at least. He definitely knows how to make a patient feel good at just the right moment. As I watch him do a procedure I am sure he performs numerous times a day, I can't help but notice how inviting and friendly he is. The procedure is uncomfortable, but his attentiveness and humor make me feel like I'm not alone, and he genuinely cares about my health and making me feel comfortable. I really need that.

Christmas tree. Haha. The dye that they have just inserted will have my entire left side glowing. They are going to be able to see my lymph nodes and breast area a lot clearer on these screens. Hopefully it gives them more insight on how to quickly tackle this unwanted visitor.

I'm listening as this lady gives me a full warning on how the tube may cause anxiety, especially if I'm claustrophobic, and aIso on the importance of being completely still while in the tube so they can get great pictures of the lymph nodes and breast area.

How small is this tube?

Anytime I am given instructions on how to remain safe when dealing with equipment or something that could potentially harm me, I instantly become nervous, but for some reason this time was a little different. I was actually looking forward to the stillness of that machine. The machine would give my body and thoughts a chance to catch up with one another. I have been so exhausted with my new life I haven't taken the time to just let my mind rest. This could be just what I needed.

As I prepare to be rolled into the tube, I can't help but think of the MRI machine as if it were a small hiding space from all of my problems and fears. It reminds me of when I was a kid and I had a space just for me and my thoughts. Imagining this machine as my hiding spot automatically helps the process fly by.

I am doing my best not to move because if I do, they might have to start these pictures over. I take a moment to reflect on where I am in life. The first questions that come to mind are, "How in the world did I get to this place? Where in life did I go wrong?" I always imagined hitting rock bottom meant being in jail or dead, but what about that step right before? Never would I have imagined being where I am, right here … right now. They are taking pictures of the very thing that is trying to kill me. I don't know how I got here. I just know I am not staying here!

Self, repeat after me, "YOU GOT THIS! YOU WERE MADE TO WIN! YOU WILL NOT BE DEFEATED! EVERYTHING WILL GO AS PLANNED! GOD HAS YOU COVERED AS HE ALWAYS DOES. YOU WILL COME OUT ON TOP!"

We're finally done with pictures, and I am finally in a space that is closed off by a curtain, waiting on the doctor to wheel me in the operating room. At this point, I don't mind waiting because I'm exhausted. I have experienced every emotion imaginable during this cancer journey so far, and I've only begun! If I am awake during my surgery, that will be fine with me. I just want to get it over with.

Ok, who is this guy, and why is he carrying around this big tank? He comes over to me, asks me for my name and information, and tells me to sign the waiver and consent forms. He then places a mask over my face and says that the anesthetic should work immediately. This mask is familiar. This is the same type of mask they use at the dentist office to give you laughing gas to help with pain, so now I'm excited because I think this will fix all of my anxiety problems.

After about five minutes, I begin to panic again because I don't feel the anesthetic taking effect! Dang it! He didn't give me enough. Of all the times he could have overdosed, me he missed the perfect opportunity. I guess I just have to face my …

***

Where am I? Who is this guy beside my bed? Why am I so tired? Is my surgery over? Already? What time is it? What happened to the doctor, and the light, and the scalpels? I didn't feel a thing. Shoot, I don't even remember going to sleep! I do feel a little sore, but I don't remember any of what happened after the weird tank man left.

The surgery was not that bad. Heck, maybe I'll do it again. I am joking of course, but seriously, it may not be so bad after all. Thank God that it is over though. Now onto the real challenge.

THE HAIRCUT

I've decided to cut my hair before I start my chemo treatments. I figure it will help my children cope with the hair loss a little better if I am proactive about introducing them to this idea of short hair. Making sure that I am in control of this process as much as I can be is important to me because I feel like the little control I have over my life is almost nonexistent.

Now, I'm very picky about my hair. The styles I always choose are always pretty simple. I have some styles picked out for the stylist who is going to cut my hair. She can help me choose. Hopefully I can pull off one of these styles without looking too masculine. I am definitely nervous about the end result, but I'm more concerned about making my children as comfortable as possible about this drastic life change than I am about my hair. After all, it will grow again eventually.

My best friend has come along with me for moral support, and the stylist is a high school classmate and friend who I trust, so I'm surrounded by people who will keep me lifted. People say, when life-changing events happen, you find out a lot about the people in your life, and that has proven to be true. As I said earlier, I consider myself to be alone, but I'm definitely overwhelmed at all the support I am receiving from friends and family members! I'm trying to be the strong one so I never have to ask these people for anything, but at this moment, I am so glad that they are not listening to me when I say I am ok. Honestly, I don't care how strong you are—we all need someone we can lean on during times like these.

***

The stylist did a great job on my hair. She gave me exactly what I asked for and what was shown in the picture. I am impressed at the fact that her skills were that good, but I'm super sad at the same time. Even though I told her I liked it, honestly, I don't. Although I refused to cry when she was cutting it, crying is definitely on my to-do list because I hate my hair.

Or maybe it isn't my hair that I hate. Maybe it is what this haircut represents: the fact that I could not stop the inevitable. Maybe what I hate is the fact that I don't think it is fair that it is me going through this. Maybe I now officially hate my life. I am forced to live from this point forward. I find my smile fading by the day, and I feel like I have nothing to be happy about. My life is a wreck and I have no control over what happens to me. Look at me—I'm trying to be strong for my children when honestly, I need someone to be strong for me.

THE FIRST DAY OF CHEMO

So today is the day I have been preparing for since I found out I have cancer, and as prepared as I thought I was, I really am not ready. I feel sick to my stomach. All of my family and friends are at the hospital waiting to support me, so I feel like I have to be super brave. I'm glad no one can see my thoughts because they would definitely check me into a mental hospital right now. I have a headache, my stomach hurts, my heart is pounding, and I want to run far, far, away from this entire situation. But where would I go to escape it? And is it worth the risk of refusing treatment? Time is not on my side. I am not in a position to take chances. I have people who need me. No turning back now.

My mom is in the car waiting for me. I have everything I need.

Ok, Self, quick pep talk.

YOU GOT THIS! YOU WERE MADE TO WIN! You will not be defeated! Everything will go as planned, and GOD HAS YOU COVERED AS HE ALWAYS DOES. YOU WILL COME OUT ON TOP!

Ok, let's go. God, lead the way.

***

That ride was not long enough. The hospital is closer than I thought. I feel like I need a few more hours of silence to prepare myself for what is behind those sliding doors.

Well, my mom just turned off the ignition, so I guess that plan is out. Here goes nothing.

Get out of the car, Lakeya, and play it cool. Don't let these people know you are afraid. Stay calm and walk forward. Fight back those tears and handle your business.

The sliding doors are opening. No turning back now!

***

Why is this place so calm? Why are these people so happy? Why is it that I am the only person who seems afraid to be here? You would think that based off of the things that these patients go through, the scenic area would be a little gloomier. I mean, I am livid by having to be in this place. I'm pretty sure that these people have just decided to accept the situation for what it is. Will I ever get to that place? I guess only time will tell.

Oh, the receptionist has no hair! She's beautiful! Even though I am afraid of that style, she is definitely pulling it off. I can't deny she looks great as a bald-headed woman. She has the perfect-shaped head for the bald look. I wonder how long she has been dealing with cancer? She's super friendly. I like her attitude, and I instantly feel like I can connect with her. I think she is perfect for this position. Even though I've been here only a few moments, she has made me feel so comfortable and welcomed. I wonder if I would be able to have this job as well when I complete my chemo. She must find her job to be rewarding, making people feel comfortable during these tough situations. They say first impressions are everything, and at this moment, I believe that. Not to mention, she gets a chance to be bald and make a statement while doing so. What a brave woman! I hope to be half as confident and beautiful as she is.[1]

Oh, what a pleasant surprise! This facility has a garden with a water fountain, which is as still as can be. The sun is shining down serenely on the beautiful flowers, and hey, there are hummingbirds in this little garden! There are benches so patients and their visitors can go out and sit to enjoy the scenery. That is definitely a plus! It's almost a little place to escape, even for just a minute, from all your problems.

Weirdly enough I think that excites me a little. It gives me the feeling of hope.

What, wait?! Is that a self-playing piano? Cool. I didn't even know that they existed anymore! The music is so calm and peaceful yet happy and energetic.

---

[1] When writing this book, I discovered that this wonderful woman was actually not a cancer patient. Her baldness was a result of alopecia.

It reminds me of elevator music, but either way it is a very nice feature.

Inside is a gift shop with a built-in beauty salon. How cool is that? There are so many wigs along the walls to choose from.

This facility is perfect. It reminds me again of a peaceful place to be. One that brings a sense of happiness to this strange, scary new world I am trying to fit into. Maybe just maybe this will not be as bad as I …

Oh, never mind. They are calling my name and I suddenly feel sick all over again. So much for that peaceful place. Back to reality. I am not prepared for what is ahead. I mean, honestly, how do you prepare mentally for chemo treatments? I can hear them calling my name, but my body is not allowing me to make a move.

My mom gives me a nod of encouragement. Without a chance to contemplate the situation anymore, I take a deep breath and drag my feet forward to move into the next level of my future destiny.

***

What's back here? Oh, another waiting room. This one doesn't feel the same. I'm going to just keep my head down in this room; it's not very welcoming.

It's reassuring that I'm not here alone though. My sister is attempting to keep me company, but I am a wreck. The longer we sit here, the more frightened I become.

Oh my goodness... are those little hats? What are they for? Why would someone have knitted hats for the upcoming spring? I guess I don't understand, but they are cute. I wonder who made them? I guess that really doesn't matter either. I am a nervous wreck, and I am rambling. I need to focus on something else.

Ok, here comes the doctor. Oh no, it is just a lady finishing treatment. Another bald head. She too is a beautiful woman, but she isn't smiling.

You know what ..., it just hit me. That is my future. Look at her. I can't imagine what she is feeling on the inside. I mean, she has no hair! That is one of the key components that makes a woman different from a man. Hair. Not only is the hair on her head missing but her eyebrows are gone as well. She looks like my perception of a cancer patient. She is walking a little slower and she doesn't fit the same category as the lady who works up front—she is really a cancer patient, and

I am a few treatments away from looking and feeling just like her.

I can't fight it any longer. I am afraid, and I can't stop these tears from falling. I want my mom and a tight hug from my kids. I want to be held. I am not strong enough for this. I am not okay. I am literally having a breakdown in a waiting room full of cancer patients. How selfish of me. But I can't stop crying.

Why me?! I mean, forgive me, but I am young; this is not something I should have to be dealing with! I haven't seen anyone under fifty since I have been at this hospital. These people have lived at least half of their lives. I want to be given the same opportunity. I am not supposed to be here. I am not a cancer patient!!

Ok, so I'm sure people now think that I'm crazy. Not only the others in the waiting room, but now this nurse who has to take care of me. I'm sure my first impression was not as welcoming as the lady up front. Poor nurse. Having to deal with other people who are sicker than me and also having to deal with adult babies like myself. I'm sure she is saying to herself, "I don't get paid enough for this." Nonetheless, she seems to be a nice lady. She's extremely professional and helpful. I can't really decide if she is the type of nurse that I had envisioned I would want, but I also don't feel bad vibes from her so I guess we'll just have to see.

This room is private. Although I don't get my own closed door, I do feel that the space is my own. My room has a TV and a reclining chair. The recliner is a nice touch. It beats laying down in a hospital bed, and I feel comfortable sitting here in it scrolling through social media. I'm grateful for the food tray stand and unlimited heated blankets. Again, thank you to the person who came up with that idea! These places can be a little cold, and being hooked up to an IV with fluids will make you even colder, so the heated blankets are especially nice.

My nurse is explaining how she will hook me up to the machines for my treatment, and I can't help but wonder how many times a day she has to give this same speech!

Ok, whoa! What a big needle! You know, I feel like I took the small needles that the doctor's office uses for granted. To any of my past doctors who I complained to about the smaller needles, let me take a moment to apologize!

***

Welp! I had to ask, didn't I? Apparently going fast is not safe. Inserting the chemo little by little ensures I am not rejecting or reacting negatively to it. I'm being nosey and trying to rush her, and the whole time she is trying to save my life.

EWWWW I can taste this stuff! It is at the back of my throat as if I am swallowing it or something. It tastes metallic. Luckily, my guardian angel told me to bring my peppermints to kill the taste. Now I understand why she made that suggestion!

I guess I don't feel horrible, but I do feel a little weak. It makes sense as to why that lady in the waiting room was moving a little slower earlier. Hold on ….

Nope, I feel dizzy and weird. I feel myself getting more tired by the second. I have to sit here for a few more hours to make sure that I am ok to go home. Maybe I will take a little nap.

***

What's that noise? Ah, it's a bell. Somebody's ringing a bell and people are clapping. What a wonderful noise! I've heard about that bell. It represents the end of your treatment! Someone has had their last chemo treatment. How wonderful for them! I am going to ring that bell when I complete my treatment. I refuse not to. I am going to ring it so hard I'm going to knock it off the wall! I can't wait for that day, but right now I am going to eat something from the lunch cart that they bring around. I'm starving!

Since we are still here waiting, the facility is providing us with lunch from the cafeteria. The lunch cart is definitely a positive for the day. The ladies who brought the cart are reading the list and asking what I will choose: sandwiches, fruit, Jell-o, chips, soda, muffins, salads, and even chocolate chip cookies. It's nice that my mom and grandma are able to get food too. These two poor ladies have been stuck here with me all day and haven't complained once. I think they enjoyed being able to watch all the game shows without an interruption! Most of the patients are asleep or too tired to make noise so it's a quiet environment.

Finally, it is time to go home. I had thought I could just stand up and walk out of here on my own, but my balance is off and I'm extremely tired. I fell back in my seat when I tried to stand up just now. The nurse and my mom and grandma are surrounding me trying to make sure I am ok. I don't like feeling helpless, but the thought of walking up that long hallway and through the parking lot is overbearing. Is this a normal feeling? Should I even be going home right now?

The nurse told me that it would get better. I have no choice but to believe her, and I'm just too tired to put up a fight about it. I refuse to look weak, though. This cancer thing will not beat me! I walked into this hospital; I will walk out!! Just a little slower. Not only is my resilience kicking in, but it is followed by pride. I am determined to not let cancer beat me.

From where I am standing, the front exit to the car seems miles away. I badly want to just turn around and hop back in the chemo chair until this process is over, or even ride in that wheelchair I was offered, but I have something to prove at this point. I can do this; I just have to put one foot in front of the other and not focus on the front door but every step I take so when I do look up it will not seem so far away. This does not seem like it's going to be a walk in the park.

Lord, I need you to help me on this journey.

***

Tonight is one to remember. My kids are not allowed to come around me for a while for their safety and mine because of the chemo, so I have decided to go home alone. I am so weak, and I don't want anyone to see me like this. I want to isolate myself from the world. My guardian angel had previously told me to make sure to potty a lot and to drink lots of water and Gatorade to offset how much fluid I was passing. She said drinking lots of fluid would make me feel better faster, so I'm doing as instructed. I have been camped out by my bathroom all night so I won't have to walk far. But I miss my children. Since they were born, I have always been Mama Bear, doing almost everything for them. Now I have to depend on my mother and their dads to oversee the primary care for them, and I absolutely hate feeling like a needy person. I have been trying to sleep off the tired feeling but it just will not leave.

I have been doing ok most of the night, but at some point a few hours ago, a feeling came over me that I wasn't prepared for. It felt like an ongoing hangover. I was dizzy with the worst headache I have ever experienced. All I could think to do was to pray.

Although my mom lives only three houses from me, I don't want her to have to watch my babies and me too. I don't want to put that much pressure on her. Being the stubborn person that I am, I am going to just sit here and fight through it. Honestly, I feel like I am going to die, and I'm terrified I will die alone. The only thing I have to hold on to at this point is my faith. I know if I'm going to make it through the night, it will be because of the big man himself.

God, please watch over me.

PART THREE

IT WASN'T A DREAM

The next morning, I called my mom super early to ask her to come and pick me up. I was so relieved to hear her car pull up to my house a few minutes later. I wanted to run and jump into her arms; I was so relieved to see her there. Although in my head I wanted to tell her to save me from all of this, I knew in reality she did not have the power to do so, and I did not want to put any more stress on her than she already had. Instead of exploding into tears as the frightened little girl that this experience has brought out of me, I chose to remain silent and tell her everything was ok. Her presence was all I could fathom to bother her with, so I took that and did not make a fuss of things. She updated me on my children's progress and assured me that they were ok. I used that reporting as my ammunition to keep going, and it was working, for the time being.

I wanted so badly for all of this to be a dream. Based on the previous night, I knew I was not going to be able to pull this whole process off alone. The worst part was, I had to take another dose of chemo that morning, only a few hours after such a horrible night the previous night, and it was a different brand.

I was a mental wreck.

Will tonight be a repeat of last night? Will it be worse?

According to my guardian angel, this particular brand would not make me as tired, but it would affect my joints and muscles. She suggested taking Claritin to offset the medicine. I did as instructed; after the previous night, I couldn't afford not to.

I was extremely tired that morning, but I had fought to get up and get dressed. I still felt I as in control of my body, but I knew that after a couple more doses of chemo, I wouldn't be able to say that would be the case.

I was all ready to go and had everything I needed, including my new best friend—my journal. I thought I should write a game plan before it was too late. It was time to make some much-needed changes.

We arrived at the hospital on time. This time the ride felt a little longer than usual. I was queasy and tired, and I could feel every bump in the road from my house to the hospital parking lot. Honestly, I was in no hurry to go in or even see the nurse, and I didn't want to be bothered. Thankfully, the doctor made me wait. I took this much-needed time to write in my journal. I had so much to say. So much to figure out without a lot of time to gather the perfect game plan. I was amazed at how the pages begin to quickly fill up. I did not realize I had so much built up inside of me the last few weeks. It felt good to have an outlet to share all of those crazy thoughts I was holding. I could feel the weight lifting off of me with every stroke of the pen. It was at that moment that I decided that this was definitely something I needed to keep doing in order to freely express myself without judgment. It is hard being a single woman and not having enough heart to put added pressure on my current support system. I wanted to keep from burning them out because I was not sure how long the cancer process would be. Finally, the nurse called my name.

I anticipated being there for hours like I had been there the day before, but surprisingly, it was a pretty short visit. The nurse gave me a shot in my upper arm area, and about fifteen minutes later, she told me I was free to go. I was so relieved, and I couldn't get out of there fast enough! All I wanted to do was lie down.

Nothing else mattered. It wasn't until I was home and comfortable that I felt the muscle pain begin to form in my arms and legs and back, making it almost impossible to lie down. I felt awful and spent most of my day sleeping in a chair.

***

I did one round of chemo every two weeks for eight weeks and another type of chemo weekly for sixteen weeks. My routine continued for a total of twenty weeks. I was miserable. As soon as the medicine wore off and I started to feel somewhat normal, it would be time for another dose. There was no relief. I was really starting to feel defeated. I was getting worn down not only physically but mentally as well. But I managed to fight through those first eight weeks the best I knew how.

I had to be honest with myself. On top of being sick and queasy all the time, I was missing work. I wasn't physically able to go. As a waitress at the time, I had to be able to stand on my feet for at least six hours a day moving nonstop. My constant weakness ruled that out. Luckily, I had a wonderful support system that really came through for me, but the reality was still there. How long could I depend on them to handle their bills and mine also? Would I be able to even go back to work? Should I send my kids off with their dads until I could fully take care of myself again? Their grades were suffering, and my son was acting out. I mean, sixth grade is already hard enough without the uncertainty of what's going on when your mom is undergoing cancer treatment. My daughter was full of questions I didn't have the answers to. My mom did a great job, but she was trying to help me on top of dealing with her own health issues.

Honestly, I couldn't bear the thought of slowly losing my kids. They are the very reasons I get up every morning. I needed my kids; however, I questioned whether I would be able to fully take care of myself again. Everything dealing with my future was so unclear. I wasn't sure of anything except that I had to make some tough decisions, and time was not on my side.

I was going to chemo weekly, so I really was not working at all. When I felt up to it, I did as much research as I could. Most of the time I just rested. I attempted to receive unemployment, but in order to do so, I had to be able to work, and no one was looking to hire a cancer patient who couldn't predict which days would be good and which would be bad. I would automatically miss at least one work day a week already because of my weekly visits to the cancer center, so that ruled out my plan to try and get my unemployment insurance. Then I tried to receive short term disability, but in order to do so, I had to not be able to work at all. I needed a doctor's note stating I was unable to work. The truth is, I was able to work, but I wasn't sure what days I would feel good enough to do so. It was a catch-22. Not only was I out of energy, but I was out of ideas as well. The only resort, and I mean my last resort, was to ask my parents if I could move in with them. At that point, I felt like I had officially hit rock bottom.

But I wasn't ready to give up hope yet. My parents agreed to let me live with them until I felt better and was able to get back on my feet. The move-in was pretty smooth. A lot of friends and family jumped in to help me out. They packed and moved my belongings for me because I wasn't really allowed to do much heavy lifting. I was overjoyed by the number of people who came to my rescue. This move was one of the many times I realized how blessed I really am to have such a great support system.

Although the move was physically easy, the mental portion of it definitely wasn't. I love my parents, but that is one of the last things you want to do as an adult—move back in. I struggled mentally because I was trying to parent my children under the same roof I was being parented under. I was definitely not in control of my everyday functions anymore, and I began to face the reality that nothing would ever be the same again.

I recall one time having to use the bathroom and just not having the strength to make it from one room to another. I was still using the methods my guardian angel had taught me, but they were definitely not as effective as they had initially been. I was sitting in a chair after drinking a lot of water. I really had to potty, but for some reason I couldn't move my legs to lift myself out of the chair. In my mind, I felt strong enough to move, but my body wasn't moving. I could literally see the bathroom door, but I couldn't move. I was too weak to stand on my own. I had to call my son to help me up out of the chair and hold me up on the toilet to potty. I was so embarrassed and broken. This one incident took a major mental toll on me and how I imagined my future would be. I didn't want my son to see me sad, so I held back my tears until he helped me back to my chair, but when I knew the coast was clear and I was alone, I let the tears flow. I cried for hours. And I cried myself to sleep in that chair.

At that moment, I could honestly say I understood why people give up sometimes. To wake up and feel that useless is a hard pill to swallow. I didn't want my kids to have to see me like that. Weak and broken. I have always been known as strong, and so I take pride in being a strong individual that they can look up to. I started to see a pattern of many different mental stages, but I was just too weak and broken to share this with anyone else. I didn't want people to think I was a threat to myself or others. It felt like those different stages mentally were taking over my life, not to mention affecting my physical health. I was waking up feeling, "What is the point? Why am I here? Would it be better if I wasn't? Would it make life easier on everyone else that was forced to take care of me if I weren't?" The truth is, I needed someone to tell me I mattered, I was needed, and I had a purpose.

Was my strength now a thing of the past? Would I ever be in control of my life again? Those weekly treatments were definitely taking a lot out of me.

TAKING BACK MY LIFE

By the fourth round of my first sixteen weeks of treatments, I was pretty used to the routine. I actually started looking forward to my visits because there were some good parts of taking treatment. I loved to visit my nurse and receive those free cookies from the cart. I loved hearing the bell, knowing that the sound meant that someone else was finishing their treatment! And I loved meeting so many new people, a lot of great people with different versions of the same story. So many people shared their stories of how they had been dealing with cancer.

I actually met an older couple, and the husband was the one with cancer. He had been dealing with cancer since 1987. That really stuck out to me because that was the year I was born! Here I was whining over my few months of treatments and he was going on thirty years' worth of treatments! It makes you view life a little differently. He was the life of the party type—always happy. Crazy, right?

The amount of time I spent in that cancer center gave me the perfect opportunity to realize that even though my life was not ideal, that didn't mean it wasn't a good life. My whole experience started to make me thankful for the things going well in my life. For instance, I became grateful for being able to walk into the hospital on my own every week. I walked past people who were too weak to walk in on their own.

And having friends and family there for every visit had such a huge positive impact on me. Some people didn't have family, so they were there alone. Their situation made me acknowledge that we all need someone; we are not meant to be on this earth alone.

By this point in my treatment, I was finally ready to accept my reality. I wanted to be like the husband I met who had been dealing with cancer almost as long as I had been alive! I wanted to bring the light with me. I wanted people to be happy when they saw me, as well. It was time that I started living my truth. It was time to again be happy in the person that I always was—a beautifully-created cancer patient fighting like hell to change that "patient" title to "survivor"! I made up my mind that I was going to live, and I was going to live my life more abundantly. Sixteen weeks was a hell of a long time, but I would not go down without a fight! Besides, I had all the help I needed. Now this journey was even more personal than before. I would be victorious! I needed to be victorious just as much as I needed to breathe. It was at this moment I knew that my surviving and completing my journey was so much bigger than me. I looked all around me and realized that these people needed a light just like that man was for me and it was time I started shining!

YOU GOT THIS, LAKEYA! YOU WERE MADE TO WIN! You will not be defeated! Everything will go as planned, and GOD HAS YOU COVERED AS HE ALWAYS DOES. YOU WILL COME OUT ON TOP!

Ok, bell get ready … here I come!

THE LOOK

The following week as my birthday, and on one of the days I was feeling good, I wanted to celebrate. I mean, you only turn thirty-two once, right? And of course, now every birthday meant so much more. So I had the perfect hair color picked out; I wanted to dye my hair pink. A soft pink and rose-gold color. It was going to be my big debut to really embrace this new look on life. I had the outfit and the shoes, just not the time to make the look happen.

On the day of my hair coloring appointment, my hair began to fall out. I didn't want to waste time or the little money I had so I canceled the appointment and chose to celebrate my birthday in a small casual setting with friends and family. Hopefully I could celebrate big as soon as all of this cancer stuff was over.

My hair started falling out in clumps at a time. My doctor warned me it was coming, and I had already mentally prepared myself for it anyway. I knew it was coming; I just had no idea as to when. Now, I found it interesting that from the books I'd read and the movies I'd seen, hair loss was mentioned, but not to the extent that it really happens. I lost every strand of hair I had! Not only on my head, either. It started down low and moved its way up. I lost arm hair, underarm hair, and even my eyebrows. I had no idea that it worked that way! I wasn't scared; I was actually intrigued by the hair loss, and I feel like I handled it pretty well.

My daughter probably struggled with it the most. She was going through a stage where having hair separated you from being a girl versus a boy, and I'm sure seeing my hair loss not only shocked but confused her. She would often offer to help me glue it back on or draw pictures of me with a bald head. Her gestures didn't make me feel good, but I understood these were her ways of coping with the weirdness of the situation. I would often take moments to shop with her for different matching headbands, and trying on wigs was something we enjoyed together, also. Those shopping trips definitely lightened the mood a lot, and I was able to spend quality time with her while making the best of the situation.

My daughter was probably my biggest introduction to the stares and sad attention I received from people who didn't understand what I was going through or know how to react to me. That type of attention was weird at first. I tried using the different beauty tips that the hospital and my friends and family offered, but I didn't feel those efforts made me authentic. It actually made me look worse, believe it or not, so I decided to be brave and embrace my bald head. I mean, how many times can you say you get to pull off the bald look? It gave me back that sense of liberation I had been searching for those past few months. Embracing my baldness made me feel like I could do anything I wanted to. It made me feel super brave, and I felt like I was ready to show the world the new and improved me.

So with this newfound confidence, I decided to post a picture of my bald head on social media. I paused for a second before I pushed the send button. I'm pretty private, so this would be the first time someone other than close friends and family would have seen me since I had been diagnosed. I bought myself a wrap that I had seen some of the Instagram models wear, and my best friend was nice enough to put some eyelashes on me, which turned out to look

AMAZING! I was really feeling like myself when I snapped the selfie. I stared at the picture for a couple of hours before I decided to post it. I had accepted the new me, but would the world do the same?

At this point it didn't matter. I was going to hit send—I needed to hit send. I needed my carefree spirit back, and I knew this was the only way to reclaim it. I was tired of being trapped in my own fears of what everyone else would think. It was time to be free.

I sent the picture, and I closed social media. Before reading what the world really thought, I needed to take in the entire winning moment I just experienced and celebrate it for myself. I was knocking down the walls that I had built over the past few months. I was feeling lighter by the minute, and I was so proud of myself. I deserved that smile that came across my face and that feeling of joy that filled my heart. I was on the path back to being a better me, and it felt really good!

Eventually, I opened my social media page back up. I was pleasantly surprised at all the love I received. Now subconsciously, I knew that some of the people showing love were definitely not being genuine, but at least I wasn't having to defend myself or deal with anyone being cruel, so I counted it as a win.

You don't realize how many people are on your social media until you experience something huge in your life and they like your photo. I had forgotten about some of these people, and they were seeing me for the first time in a long time with this bald head. I was tempted to take the picture down even though the reactions were positive, but I told myself, "Lakeya, keep the picture up. You have come too far to go backwards." I had to stand by my initial decision of adding the photo and go with it. No turning back now!

REENTERING THE WORLD

A few weeks after posting the picture, I decided it was time to explore the world a little. I was driving more and more, so one day I drove down to the Little Caesars to pick up pizza for my children. I wore a black and pink, fitted, flowered dress and a pair of glittery sandals. I tried to dress as girly as possible to reflect my old identity. I thought I pulled it off pretty well.

On the way into the Little Caesars, I saw a father and his son who had obviously had the same idea for their dinner. The father was actually a little flirty with me. He complimented me on my dress and how beautiful I looked that day. Shocked by his flirtatious comments, I graciously accepted them, thanked him, and smiled flirtatiously back to indicate that I accepted and appreciated the much-needed attention. He held the door for me as I walked into the building. I received many stares, but the guy's kind words kept me in a good mood and helped me steel myself against the unwanted attention. The guy's son had to be around six years old based on his size and how impatient he was waiting for the pizza.

We didn't have to wait long for our pizza. Once we were completely checked out and on the way out the door, I heard the little boy say to his dad, "She looks like a man!" Honestly, I was a little unprepared for the kid's honesty, but I acted as if I didn't hear him and continued out the door. The dad was shocked by his son's response and I could tell he was a little embarrassed. I expected him to apologize for his son's comment and that would be the end of it but no, he picked his son up and told him, "Son there is nothing manly about her. That is the definition of a beautiful woman." And then he said to me, "Keep shining, Queen!"

My cheeks hurt from how much I was smiling! I couldn't have asked for anything more. The very moment I thought I was going to go back into my shell made me toss that shell aside. I was more confident than ever, all thanks to this kind man's words.

I walked to my car with my head a little higher and my chest out a little farther. This man had given me what I needed. Another victory on this journey! I couldn't have been happier. What's next?

THE BELL

One treatment away from completing chemo. Wow! I had made it to the other side of the bell. No longer was I listening to others celebrate their completion. It was now my turn! The time had come! I don't know if that makes me more nervous or excited. I was so focused on ringing the bell, I allowed that to be my main focus to keep me pushing through my treatments. Now that the bell-ringing ceremony was here, would I lose focus on all the other treatments? I wondered what my drive would be now?

Once I finished my chemo, I still had to take radiation treatments, so my cancer journey was not done but I was officially ready to ring the bell signifying my completion of chemo treatments. Now, from the moment I had heard that bell ring during my first chemo treatment, I had held onto my ongoing prayer to God.

Lord, please allow me the strength and opportunity to ring that bell.

I believed I was going to ring that bell no matter how long it took, and I had finally made it to that very moment. All of my friends and family came out to support me during this time, and I was beyond grateful for the turnout. Honestly, I felt a little selfish because I had friends and family members take off work to show up for me at that moment. This generous act reaffirmed for me that my support system was nothing less than amazing!

Although the ringing of the bell was a personal ceremony, there was more than one patient scheduled to do it, so I had to wait my turn. Fifteen minutes away from the freedom I had been working towards for months, I was smiling and enjoying friends and family, but I was a nervous wreck on the inside. I was anxious and impatient. I wanted time to hurry up so it would be my turn. I wanted to shake the bell off of that wall! More than anything, I wanted to be free of my current situation, and I thought that bell was the answer to all of my problems.

The nurse called my name, and I was ready! I walked towards the bell with my head held high. I was prepared for this bell ringing. I had had a dress made that read *Beauty Beats Beast*, and I was wearing it proudly. I was ready to go back to my normal life. All I had to do was walk up and ring this bell, and voila, life would be as I remembered!

I walked up to that bell, gave my speech, and thanked everyone for coming. As my fingers touched the string to ring the bell, I felt a burst of energy flow through me. I didn't want to let go of the string. If I could have, I would have rung that bell all day with no consideration for the other patients.

When I said that this journey was personal, I meant just that. I was on a planet of my own for the entire day. I could not believe that I had come so far. Nothing and no one could bring my spirits down this day. This was hands down one of the best days of my life.

I did it! We did it! God did it! I was officially done with that chapter in my life. No more chemo! No more tiredness and grogginess. I was done! Thank you, God! No more horrible taste in my mouth, no more hour-long entrapments behind those curtains, no more constant needles, no more unwelcomed naps, no more fear of the next treatment, no more uncertainty of tomorrow, no more pain. I was done with it all! Thank you, God, for answering my prayers and delivering me right on time!

PART FOUR

RADIATION

A week into what I thought was normal life, I began to see that normal life as I knew it was never to be again. I was in constant pain, and I was still extremely fatigued. I wanted to crawl out of my body and start life fresh somewhere else.

I had imagined that by this time, I would at least be preparing to go back to work. Others had told me that radiation was a lot easier than chemo. I wasn't concerned about whether it would be better or not. I planned to handle it as I do all my situations—just make the best of it and keep pushing through. There were thirty rounds of radiation that I was preparing for, meaning I would take a round of radiation every day for thirty days.

(Deep breath) You can do this, Lakeya! Thirty days or take a chance on the cancer coming back.

The process was totally different from what I imagined it to be. I expected there would be lasers like they use during laser tag, loud noises, and a lot of beams lighting up all over the place. I wasn't 100 percent wrong. There was definitely a laser beam, but it was a huge one that hung from the ceiling. It was a tube-shaped object, and I was afraid it would shoot a hole right through me!

The first couple of visits were long and drawn out. The radiologist prepared me for the treatment, which only lasted about fifteen minutes, but the process was still a mental challenge. Once I was undressed, they would place me on a straight board that held me still while the laser was doing its thing. I wasn't sure how the laser would feel during that first treatment. I have to admit, I was pretty afraid, but I knew in order to get to thirty I had to start with one.

The ladies that were helping left the room and went behind a glass shield. From there, they proceeded to talk to me. Of course, this made me feel awkward wondering why they were leaving me there to receive this radiation if they knew it wasn't safe enough for them to be in the same room! I felt myself getting sick so I closed my eyes and said a short prayer. After the prayer, I was still a little uneasy so I started to recite my now-famous chant:

YOU GOT THIS! YOU WERE MADE TO WIN! You will not be defeated! Everything will go as planned, and GOD HAS YOU COVERED, AS HE ALWAYS DOES. YOU WILL COME OUT ON TOP!

The technicians behind the glass turned the lights down low and informed me they were about to begin. I could see the laser tube machine start to move. It was a lot quieter than I imagined. I was envisioning the people behind the glass controlling the laser as if it were the crane machine button that you see in the arcade to catch the stuffed animals. During the preparation process, they had placed sticky circles on me to instruct the laser where to shoot. The laser moved slowly towards the circle conveniently placed on the left side of my chest. The machine stopped, and the laser shot a beam at its target. The laser didn't feel weird as I imagined it would; honestly, I didn't even feel a thing. They controlled the laser, placed it over the sticky circles, aimed, and shot. I was out of there in less than thirty minutes.

I was relieved that this process was not as bad as chemo. Maybe I could handle this after all. I didn't feel tired afterwards, and I was relieved that radiation would not add to the pain I was already trying to shake. The treatments started to fly by.

The crew that was helping me was younger, so we were able to relate more during those awkward conversations. Social media and Trump gave us enough fodder to fill those gaps. I met some amazing people during this time, many of which I still call my Pink Sisters. I had met some of them previously during chemo, but patients are not able to talk as much during chemo treatments. I would see them daily now, so it was easier to establish relationships and get to know who they really were. So many beautiful and intelligent ladies from all walks of life. I met teachers, home interior decorators, nurses. I even ran into some old classmates! I was amazed at how many people were affected by this disease and going through the same experience that I was.

After the first couple of weeks, I had a routine. I would go a couple of minutes early to talk with my newfound friends, prepare for the daily treatment, and leave promptly after the treatment. All was going well until about three weeks in when I began to feel a burning sensation around my breast. I wasn't alarmed at first. The way that it appeared made me think it was a rash. It started out red and itchy with a little bit of pain and discomfort. I informed the nurse about it, but she told me it was normal, so I just let it go. By the end of that week, that burning sensation had worsened and my skin had started peeling. The radiation had caused my skin to peel and made the entire left side of my breast to appear to be raw. Just flesh.

The rash also had a smell to it. The radiation had caused my skin to melt. I was starting to panic because I wasn't aware of the danger of my skin melting and the pain that came along with that. The doctor thought it was a good idea to wait a couple days to allow it to heal a little before continuing treatment. I was devastated! How could that little laser cause so much damage to my skin? Now it made sense as to why the technicians went behind the glass. Can't say that I blame them.

Once again, I began to see a discolored pattern appear in my breast. My breasts were two different colors; only one side was being treated, so the one being treated was a lot darker than the other side on the top, but the bottom was completely skinless. This was another mental setback for me because I was afraid that the color would never be the same. I also developed a burned area on my neck.

I had so many questions for my radiation doctor. How long would this pain last? Would my skin ever come back? Would those burned spots lighten up? What long-term issues would I potentially face? What if it didn't heal—how would I be able to finish my treatments?

Even though I smiled so others wouldn't notice, I was depressed. I knew stopping treatment was the best thing to do in order to heal, but I just wanted to push on and be done with this phase in my life.

This was harder than I thought.

God give me strength.

UNEXPECTED HOPE

While waiting to heal and barely being able to get out of bed, I received a phone call that helped me cope with my current situation. It was one of the counselors at the cancer center. She called and told me my chemo nurse and some of the other staff at the hospital had recommended me to be in the annual Cancer Survivors Fashion Show. She wanted to know if I wanted to be a part of this event. Without even thinking I blurted out, "Yes!"

How exciting! Just like that, I felt like I had purpose again. Now, I am not the model type, but I was definitely confident in my new walk, so this gave me a chance to strut my stuff. This opportunity felt like a continuation from ringing that bell; it was another celebration of my success so far. It gave me a sense of liberation and a chance to show my artistic side.

I was informed that I had to prepare a speech, and our local Belk store was supplying us with the outfits. What a quick turnaround in life! Although I was upset about my setback with radiation and all of the pain it was causing, I was excited to be part of something bigger than me and something so positive. I planned for weeks as to what to say, how to walk, and even how to smile. Without a doubt, practicing my speech and my smile kept me busy and kept my mind off of radiation. I planned to use this as a stepping stone back towards happiness.

FINDING PURPOSE IN PAIN

Today was the big day of the annual Cancer Survivors Fashion Show, and I could hardly wait for it to begin. I had been preparing for this day for a while. Although I had a certain vision in my head as to how I wanted to dress, I had to work with the clothing items I had been given, so I was not able to perfect my vision, but I still thought I did pretty well at pulling off the themed look.

There were nine contestants, some of which I knew from the cancer center. Two of the contestants were women I had grown fond of; one was my daughter's grandma! (Her dad's mother.) Crazy, right? Others were new to me. All beautiful and intelligent ladies who brought fire to that stage.

I arrived early because the organizers provided a makeup artist for us, so I wanted to make sure I was there in enough time to get my makeup done. When I walked into the building, I was overtaken by the decorations. Everything, and I do mean everything, was pink. Drapes, tablecloths, napkins, glasses. They even had pink wine. Now, if you know me, you know one my favorite colors is pink, so I automatically lit up! It felt like a dream.

There was a photo booth with lots of pink props, fun games set up to play, and my favorite of the night—pink gift bags filled with lots of goodies! It was breathtaking, and I had not even made it backstage yet! Some of the women arrived before I did so I had plenty of time to get to know the other ladies and wrap my head around what was really happening. The stage and number of people present were more than I had imagined, so of course the nervous bug showed up.

We were greeted in the back with another gift bag, and they catered to us as if we were royalty. We had wine, grapes, and cheese, and they offered plenty of assistance with anything we needed. There were women of all ages. One of the ladies I met was a teacher, and she was younger than me. Our profiles were similar as she had two children as well, but she was a teacher and married. She had short, fine hair like me, and her hair was also starting to grow back. She was tall and slender, and she had big beautiful eyes that stood out from her other features. She was pretty quiet, but although she didn't say much, something about her energy made her stand out.

There was also another lady who was in the early stages of chemo, and she seemed to be a little weaker than some of the other survivors. She did a lot of sitting during our session of getting dressed, but she was definitely not overlooked. Her smile stood out for me; it was bold and energetic and full of love. While waiting on makeup, we talked a lot about where she was on her journey, and I was even able to share with her some of the tips I had been given in that stage of my journey. I didn't realize it at that moment, but sharing my experiences with her gave me a sense of the purpose I had been searching for my entire life. I was able to give insight on something so much bigger than me and share the joyous feeling with this lady of simple gratitude from a conversation. We talked until it was time to get my makeup done.

My friends and I had experimented with lashes on me so I was sure I wanted the makeup artist to add lashes. The lady watched in excitement as the makeup artist placed the lashes on my eyes. I could tell she wanted to step out and be bold, but she was afraid of how it would make her look with her being an older lady. So I encouraged her to just go for it. You only live once, and if we are to learn anything from this experience, it is to live life to the fullest. Plus, I thought she could pull them off. She nervously agreed to try some for the night.

Once the makeup artist finished my makeup, I stuck around to compliment the older lady through the process of getting her lashes on, and of course they looked great! It definitely gave her a drive, and she was no longer sitting. I was so happy for her overcoming that shyness and stepping out of her comfort zone— just living life as a free woman for the night! What a feeling for her and me both! It really made me feel good to know that exemplifying and encouraging bravery in others has such a huge effect on so many people. From that moment on, I knew I wanted that to be a part of my story. Being an inspiration to others was connected to my purpose, and I planned to see that purpose through.

As time grew closer to getting on the stage, the action behind the scene started to speed up. Everyone was doing their last-minute prep for the runway. The organizers had a table for us to sit for dinner before the show started and enjoy the show while we were not on the runway. Once I was seated, I looked around the room for any familiar faces in the audience. There were so many people there. All the seats looked filled, and even a couple of people were standing. My friends and family really came out to support me! They filled two tables! I was excited to see each and every one of them. It was definitely a special moment I will remember for the rest of my life.

The show began and the announcers started naming people one by one to walk the runway. They gave a brief description of who each person was, and they read the models' bios aloud, finishing up by describing the pieces each model was wearing for the night. I was so nervous to walk that runway, but I knew that was a once in a lifetime experience so I sucked it up and strutted my way down the aisle. I could only faintly hear what the announcer said about me because I was so distracted by all the lights and cameras flashing in my face. All I knew to do was smile big and walk proud. And I did just that!

People were smiling back at me and clapping. It made me feel wonderful, like a superstar for the night! There was one guy taking a picture. I wasn't sure who he was, but he was close to the stage so I assumed the photo would be for the cancer center's website. So I smiled big! The announcers finished my bio, and I went to sit down and enjoy watching everyone else go up.

I really enjoyed this event. After everyone walked the stage, we ate dinner, and it was delicious! I had no idea healthy food could taste that good! That dinner really opened up a door for me to make healthier eating choices.

We played games and had a speaker who told her story of remembering being in our shoes and how life had changed for her since her treatment. I remember telling myself I wanted to be like her and share my story with others, as well, and one day soon I would do just that.

Once the event was over, my children ran over to me and gave me the biggest hug! They told me I looked beautiful and they were proud of me. That made me feel so good. My family and friends joined in shortly after, and I was able to mingle and take pictures that I will keep forever. I was so overjoyed on that day. I didn't want it to end because I knew that I would go back to my normal life after that.

I slept well that night because being on the runway gave me a sense of purpose again, and even though I was still in the storm, I planned to weather it out the rest of the way. I knew that if I didn't complete my story, I wouldn't have one to tell. I had to go through the tough times to appreciate the good times. I was prepared for what was to come: the last of my radiation, and surgery to follow. Once again, I had a positive outlook on life and the great things to come.

FINISHING RADIATION

The next day I was scheduled to start my radiation treatments again to work towards finishing my thirty rounds. I was more prepared this time than I had been the week previous. I was excited to see everyone because I knew they had been at the cancer survivors' event the night before. All of the staff and patients had been the first to get tickets, and it was a sold-out event.

While preparing to go for my treatment, my mom called and told me that I was on the front page of the newspaper, along with one of my favorite Pink Sisters! I was so shocked! I was trying to figure out how the newspaper got this picture. Then it hit me—the man at the front, closest to the stage. He wasn't there for the cancer center website; he was there for our local newspaper. What a pleasant surprise!

How rewarding is it to be on the front of the newspaper! God is so awesome. He allows us to shine even in our darkest moments.

I was excited! I was going to pick up a copy of the paper on my way to treatment, but social media beat me to it. All of my friends and family were sending me screenshots of my picture in the morning paper and congratulating me and showing so much love. Just to think, a couple of weeks earlier I thought I had hit rock bottom once again, and the little gesture of inviting me into an event turned into a complete celebration. What a mighty God we serve! This act of kindness from my peers and support system really put some pep in my step. That same smile I saw on the lady with the lashes was on my face the very next day. I got dressed just a little faster that day, and I even put on my best outfit to continue to indulge in that moment.

When I arrived at the cancer center, I was greeted by the beautiful bald lady at the front desk, who was holding a fresh copy of that day's paper. She had taken the liberty of grabbing a copy for me. I was so thankful that she thought of me in that moment and gave me something I could keep forever. It was so sweet. Everyone I passed was talking about how happy I looked in that picture. The front desk ladies, the ladies that take my temperature, the nurses, the radiologist ladies, even the doctor. I felt like a local celebrity. I used this energy to get through that thirty-minute treatment. It made the time fly by. I was there for over an hour but only spoke with people about the event mostly.

***

One treatment turned into five, and before I knew it, I was back in my routine going for daily treatments. Eventually the pain returned, but by then, I was a couple of treatments from being done so the doctor decided to just finish treatments instead of stopping again.

The radiation really took a toll on my joints. I was not feeling well and I stopped pretending as if I was. Finally, after the last treatment, I was able to ring yet another bell, but this one didn't feel the same. No longer did that bell represent freedom for me; it was now a representation of only the next levels to come. God help me.

***

The pain continued over my next few doctor's visits, which led me to physical therapy for a treatment called *iodine*. Iodine is a liquid treatment that physicians generally use on your hands and feet. They wrap your hands and feet in a plastic wrap and place these glove-like wraps over your hands and feet. Once the wraps are placed, the doctor lets them heat up. I'm not sure how the iodine enters your skin, but somehow it does. They have you sit in recliners and remain as still as possible for the time allotted to you, whether it is thirty minutes or an hour. It reminded me of being in the nail shop when you are drying your hands and feet at the same time.

I was hoping that this iodine treatment would work because I'd been experiencing a lot of trouble with my joints lately. The feeling was a constant burning sensation, and according to the doctor, some people are fortunate enough to get rid of it and some are not. In addition to preparing for this iodine treatment I had been researching things to do to occupy my time since I was no longer taking daily treatments. I was ready to start working again, but I was waiting to be released by my doctor in order to start back to work. In my little town, there are not many things I could do, but I did find a program that allowed me to get out of the house twice a week and even offered me discounts at our local YMCA. It is called Cancer Survivors Class. The class was created for people who had completed their cancer journey or are currently going through it. It is an interesting program. It offers low-impact workouts to stay in shape, and it also teaches you how to breathe properly while working out. The class reminded me of a low-impact yoga class.

I wasn't thrilled about this class, but since I started my cancer journey, I had definitely gained a lot of weight and I was low on options, so I gave it a try. The first day of class, I walked in feeling confident, knowing that I would be at the top of my class. I knew that even though I had joint pain, I was still capable of moving around pretty well, and I also knew that most of the people I knew with cancer were older so it probably would be hard for them to move at a fast pace.

I walked into the room and sat down in the front. As expected, the majority of the people in the class were at least thirty years older than me. I didn't expect to enjoy this class, but I had made a commitment to finish this class so I decided to stay. We started the class doing an evaluation as to where we were strength wise and endurance wise, whether we could keep our balance or not … the normal checklist. One of the tests was to walk to a line about twenty feet away and walk back, continuing this exercise for one minute. I was paired with a lady who was a little older than me, but not by much. She had medium-cut hair and was a pretty friendly lady from my observation of her speaking with others.

The instructors told us to begin walking, and I tried to power walk to make myself look good. To my surprise, this woman was not going to let me show her up! She started power walking as well and gave me a run for my money! So now we were in competition! Forget low impact—I now had something to prove! The faster I walked, the faster she walked. I was quickly regretting trying to be a show off because even though it was only one minute that we had to walk, I was already ready to quit after only a few seconds. I had worked up a sweat and needed water. I looked over at this woman, and she was tired too but definitely had the energy to go as long as I did. We finally made it to one minute, and we both started laughing. She had given me a run for my money, and it made me instantly like her.

I asked her what her name was and asked about her story. Ironically, she was dealing with the same cancer as me, but she had finished her treatments a little sooner than I did. It's amazing how we connected so quickly and how easy it was to talk to her. We shared our stories, and she shared some tips with me that could help me at the stage I was currently at. From that moment forward we were joined at the hip. In every team activity, we worked together, and we were always seated close enough to reach one another. She was my instant twin. I started out a know-it-all, and by the end of class I had a twin and four new mother figures. Lol.

I started looking forward to going to these classes. After trying to show off with all my tests, I then learned that the goal was to be able to beat our current scores from day one by the end of the class, so each class, I had to work hard to prove myself once again. That's what I get for prejudging this class! I also underestimated these older ladies; they were fierce and were forces to be reckoned with. I was tired after attending this class, but these ladies were doing two other classes the same day! Some were swimming, and others were doing clog and dance classes. There was even a lady who ran every day after class! They would be in these classes as early as 5 a.m. I was not that dedicated, but I definitely respected these ladies who were.

Eventually this class came to an end and we were considered graduates. The YMCA and our instructors even had a special ceremony for us that consisted of Chick-fil-A, cake, and a dance during which we had to do the chicken dance. Although I could have skipped that silly chicken dance, I was grateful for all the lifelong relationships I had made during these sessions. Everyone had friends and family that came and supported their graduate, but I had decided to take that journey alone. It was a very humbling and eye-opening experience that taught me to never judge a book by its cover and to take advantage of the opportunities that are presented to us with an open heart and mind.

Once again, I was faced with this word *survivor*, and I still wasn't sure if that is what should be used to describe me. Although I looked and felt different, I wasn't sure that I was. I knew that I had overcome a lot of obstacles since the beginning of this journey, but I was still feeling the aches and pains that came along with this cancer title. So many other people viewed me as a survivor, but I couldn't do the same for myself. Was it something that I was missing?

Am I really a survivor?

I was still feeling the sickness and dealing with the aftermath of the disease, so had I really earned that title? I wasn't convinced yet that *survivor* was the correct terminology to describe me, seeing as though I had a lifetime of healing to do in order to repair all of the parts of me that had been broken. I was definitely too invested not to keep pushing for that perfect moment as to when would be the perfect time to be described as a survivor.

As time passed, I continued to meet with my doctor for progression check-ins to make sure I was still doing well after my chemo and radiation treatments. Because I was a triple negative cancer patient, again, meaning they were not sure how I would react to any of the chemo they gave me, they hadn't removed the lump inside my breast before starting treatment. Instead, they monitored how the lump reacted to the chemo. So technically, everything up to that point had been a trial-and-error phase for me.

During my most recent visit, I was able to go back to the original doctor who had told me I had cancer. He viewed my chart and examined my breast where I was receiving treatment. He never really smiled or showed emotion, so I had to wait until he spoke before I knew how he was feeling and what he was thinking.

After a long pause he said to me, "Well I think that you are something like a miracle. In all my years of working, I have never seen a treatment work so well. It looks like you never had cancer. You are a lucky girl."

That made me smile so big, I no longer felt angry with this man because of our first encounter. In fact, I wanted to leap up off of that seat and kiss the man, I was so happy! I couldn't have gotten any better news that day.

I was so mentally drained from being stuck between having a normal life and getting acquainted with this new life. I wanted to start working again, but I also knew I had to continue to go to doctor visits until I was formally released. It was hard being patient and not really being in control of my entire life, but the news that this doctor had just given me was definitely a game changer.

He then told me that he was ready to schedule my final surgery for the removal of the dead scar tissue in my breast, which was left from the chemo and the removal of my port.

I have been awaiting this day for a few months now and it has finally arrived! Thank you, God, for your grace and mercy! I have finally been released to take back my life! What an awesome gift you and this doctor have given me! This is even better than that apology I was waiting on.

After he finished with the checkup, I got dressed and headed to the scheduling room to book my final surgery.

The lady behind the desk was so friendly. I hadn't been able to see that the first time I was there because I had been caught up in my own mess. She told me she remembered me from January, when I had come for my first appointment, and she had been concerned about me because of the way I left her office. She told me that when I left, she prayed for me and she just believed that God would take care of me. Thank God there are still some good people in this world! That was a bittersweet moment for me. I felt horrible about being rude to her and the way I had left. I was truly not in a good place mentally. At the same time, I felt so warm inside that she took the time out to pray for me. I find it amazing that we never know who is silently watching out for us. There is a lesson I learned in that moment, which is to always try to be kind even though it can be a difficult task when you are going through things. You never know who is watching.

I told her what the doctor had told me, and I also apologized to her for how I behaved the first time we met. She told me I didn't have to apologize. I told her I was glad that she was such a forgiving person and I believed she was a real child of God because of her selfless actions. We talked for a while about her family and the beautiful picture she had in her office of her children and family. She gave me my final surgery date and hugged me so tight I could feel her love through that hug. I told her I appreciated everything she had done for me and the person she was choosing to be. Her kindness lifted my spirits that day and I wasn't even aware I needed them to be lifted. Her choosing to be a kind person changed my outlook on that office. I believe I was exactly where I was supposed to be that day when I found out I had cancer.

I walked out of that office feeling like I was on top of the world. One more step in my journey and I could finally get back to my normal life.

PART FIVE

THE FINALE

After weeks of waiting, it was finally surgery day. For some reason I was not as afraid of this surgery as I was my previous one. I think I was overtaken by the adrenaline of finally being done with everything. No more treatments, no more weekly doctor visits, no more bells, no more next steps. Just pure completion and the freedom to start getting my life back to the way it once was.

I was early, as usual, so that I could check in and prepare myself for the day ahead. My mom was there with me as she had been my entire cancer journey. What a lucky person I was to have that type of support behind me!

Once I was checked in, I took a seat in the lobby until they called my name. It wasn't a long wait. It was 6 a.m., so there weren't many patients there. A nurse brought me a wheelchair so I could be rolled up to my room, but because I had the ability to walk on my own, I decided to do so. Walking down the aisle to my outpatient room made me realize how blessed I really was. I was able to choose whether I walked or had someone escort me. Although it was a little far, I wasn't out of breath or needing additional assistance. I was finally doing things that a few months prior I had only dreamed of doing. Going through cancer treatment definitely humbles you and makes you grateful for the small things in life like walking and talking, and even movement of the body with no pain. I had missed most of what my mom and the nurse were saying because I was too deep in thought about my current accomplishment and how proud I was of the growth.

Finally, we made it to the pre-op room. I was able to undress myself and tidy up my room before I had to get in bed to be pushed down that long hallway again. This time, my thought process was totally different. I was eagerly anticipating seeing the friendly little lady who came and picked me up and pushed me down to surgery. I had so much to say this time around.

That ride to the surgery area went by so quickly. I was excited to see the random people in the hall and all the nurses and doctors who were preparing me for surgery. Most of all, I was excited to see Mr. Tank Man (the anesthesiologist). Mr. Tank Man was back again for me to sign some documents agreeing before surgery that I could take the anesthesia. I signed that paperwork so fast! I was ready and weirdly a little excited to go under the knife one final time so I could get back to my life ....

***

The surgery was over. I was finally awake, and I saw that the man who watches you and alerts you to what has happened as you wake up was beside my bed again. I wasn't as shocked this time to see him. I was actually glad to see him because that meant I would be going home shortly. I would be able to spend uninterrupted time with my children and finally make plans for my life that didn't include coming to this place.

I was a little sore and it felt weird to no longer have my port inserted, so I had to get used to that, but it wasn't an awful adjustment. I could see the scar where the port had been. I wasn't thrilled to have that scar, but I would proudly wear it knowing that my overall situation and the outcome could have been much worse.

Once the man beside my bed cleared me to go back to my outpatient room, I was transported back by a strong guy. With this strong man, I didn't feel like I wasn't carrying my weight. I actually felt like royalty and I was being catered to. Maybe the hospital had heard my request about hiring strong men to transport me back and forth. Either way, I was still happy about being one step closer to home.

This was it. This was the finale, and I was as excited about the finale as I had always imagined myself to be. I looked forward to spending so much-needed time with my children, friends, family, and even myself. I was ready to create some type of normal life so that I could cope with what was to come—my life after cancer.

I remained in my room until the doctor came, checked out my scar, and made sure I was stable enough to leave. Immediately after I got the ok, I got up and started getting dressed. This time I was not fighting that wheelchair. I graciously accepted, and we were on the way to my mom's car to go home.

It was definitely bittersweet to be taking that route back home as we had done almost every day for the past six months or so. As my mom drove, I reflected on all that had happened in that half year.

I would miss the weird smell of that place and the friendly or not so friendly faces I saw daily. The wonderful staff at the hospital and my fellow cancer patients, many of whom have become lifelong friends. The peacefulness of the rooms, because most of the patients were asleep, and the sound of the bell that offered instant freedom to all of the survivors. And the cookies—yes, I would definitely miss the cookies!

I would not miss the feeling of defeat every time the chemo would be given, the medicine, the waiting process to see different doctors, the weekly and daily shots to check my vital signs, the sad faces of other patients not feeling well, and the feeling of being powerless and hopeless because I couldn't heal not only myself but everyone around me who I had grown to love.

AFTERWORD

Although I don't wish this journey on anyone, I do pray that the people having to endure this process are as lucky and blessed as I am to have such a positive ending to my story. It's amazing how your mindset determines your journey.

I vowed to myself, God, and others that I would devote my time, once I was healed, to healing others and bringing positivity, and that is what I plan to do.

From the eyes of your average person, I'm sure I was considered to be a scared, lost, confused, young, hopeful, patient who was unaware of the destiny of her future, but from behind the eyes of this cancer patient, I am a brave, coachable, self-aware warrior whose faith moved mountains! It was during this journey that I learned about the real quality of life and how your perception of it determines the outcome of how good or bad life is for you. Some of the things I experienced were the true meanings of love, happiness, faith, hope, strength, prayer, teamwork, courage, and life.

I am now ready and willing to call myself a survivor. I deserve it.

Made in the USA
Columbia, SC
26 November 2021

49731677R00067